A little Yoga Everyday

A little Yoga Everyday

A 14-day practical guide to integrating the philosophy of classical yoga into your everyday life.

by Bryony Giboin

Dedicated to my sisters and my mum for being
my biggest fans.
And Dino for always telling me I can.

Table of Contents

Introduction

1

"You don't even know how lucky you are." These were the words that ran through my ears as I sat weeping tears of pain and frustration at the feet of my meditation teacher in Bali. He was a jolly man who always smiled and laughed into his Buddha belly that shook beneath his robes. He looked at me in this moment and said these words, which I knew on the surface but didn't really understand.

I did not think I was lucky at this time in my life. I was very sick, suffering from clinical depression, an under-active thyroid, gut issues leading to vomiting when I ate, weight problems, eating problems, anxiety, acne, liver problems, adrenal fatigue, and the list goes on and on. I was not well, and I was unhappy. I hated myself.

I was in my early twenties and living a prosperous life in London—great job, great social life—but beyond the mask of ticked boxes on the lists of "should haves," I was plagued with what I used to call my dark and twisty. My dark and twisty were my deep thoughts and feelings that I would torment myself with. "You are ugly"; "No one likes you"; "Don't eat that, you will get fat"; "No one will love you if you are not skinny"; "You are not good enough for love" -- my dark and twisty I was so plagued by these and other thoughts that I couldn't be alone for fear of myself. It didn't matter how many things I bought myself; the purchases never made the smiles real. I remember one day I had just moved to a new apartment in London, I had unpacked, I had money in the bank thanks to a fantastic job, great clothes, friends, and a social life, and my health was better at this point. I lay down on my fresh sheets and thought to myself, I'm still not happy.

It was at this moment that I knew I was not living my truth. So I asked myself, "What do I want? Of course, I knew the answer already; the answer was that I wanted to travel. I had known this and dreamed about it for the past 5 years or so, but I was always saying to myself," When I have this." "Make that" or "Do this," I will go. At this very moment, I knew they were excuses that I was making to block my own happiness. Eight months later, I embarked on the biggest journey of my life. The journey of finding me.

I went from place to place, meeting one beautiful soul after another, each teaching me more and more, each holding a place in my heart. I studied and unlearned; I conditioned and reconditioned, and after graduating from my first yoga teacher training, I stepped into silence. I made a commitment to be still and to be with myself. It was the most healing and life-changing thing I ever did, but it was also the hardest thing I ever did. Not the silence, surprisingly, that was the easiest part, but being while just breathing—that is the hardest part. To be with no purpose other than to be. It was in the silence that my teacher said these words to me, "You don't even know how lucky you are," that struck me to change, accept, and apply to become who I am today, and I am proud to say that I love myself. I appreciate my trials; no, I love them, for they have made me a strong and yet a soft woman of love, wisdom, and understanding.

This book is for you to take your happiness into your own hands through the teachings of yoga because a dear friend once said to me "You are so selfish. You have all this knowledge and understanding, and it is your duty to share it". Sometimes we all need a kick in the behind to put us on our path...

I have dedicated my life to yoga and the incredible teachings that this ancient philosophy has to offer each and every one of us. Please do not think that I am referring to the pictures you see of people bending into extreme formations of their physical body, I am referring to the teachings that get lost behind this facade. The teachings that you can apply to every second of your life and not just for 60 minutes a couple of times a week. This book is to help you take yoga and make it a lifestyle, not just an exercise. Everything in this book I practice daily; I live my life to meet each moment; I take yoga off the mat and into the world; and I want to guide and share with you my secrets to creating a life of happiness, wellness, and magic that you deserve.

How to use this book

2

Think of this book like a cake. You can not just throw all the ingredients into the mixing bowl at once and think it will create a masterpiece. It just doesn't work like that!

First, you have to have the idea to bake the cake; then, you gather each ingredient one at a time, and they are mixed together bit by bit, but you ADD to the mix, not take it away.

Each day we will look at a new yogic principle, and the task is to apply it as if it were a key ingredient in the ingredients of a cake, and so to speak, it is a key ingredient in creating a life of balance! The important thing to remember is to continue to add. Once we practice one topic, our practice is not to then forget about it the next day but to continue to apply it and then add the next ingredient into the mix.

I have designed the book to add a new ingredient every day; however, sometimes ingredients need to marinade. Remember, this is your life; if you find that you need to marinate on a certain concept, then take the liberty to do just so, but don't get stuck on perfection! We don't have to be perfect at something; trying is enough.

If you are a night reader, then read the chapter for the next day before going to bed; if you are a morning reader, then read the chapter for your day first thing in the morning before setting out on your task and day!

Do this book once, then do it over and over again until it becomes second nature, like breathing. We don't have to think about it; it just happens, and life is all the more beautiful for it.

Yoga Sutras

3

....

We will mostly be using the teachings of Patanjali to help us on our journey to creating a life of expansion, so it is important that we take a moment to learn some history, a favourite subject of mine.

The word *yoga* has many meanings; in fact, if you were to ask each of your friends what it means to them, I am sure they will all have their own interpretation of this four-letter word, giving it a truly personal meaning. The root of the word *yoga* is yoke, meaning to bind, come together, or unify, and although classical yoga is not a religion, it has combined the teachings of many different religions to create a path of unity.

In around 200 BC, the book of yoga *sutras* (threads) was created as a path to *Samadhi* (bliss) by the unknown author Patanjali in India. It is not a book of religion but 196 aphorisms combining the teachings of yoga from various texts as a way to unshackle ourselves from the suffering that *we* create. The sutras are a path to ecstasy and freedom.

The most widely used concept taken from this book is the *Ashtanga* (eight) system. Not to be confused with the dynamic physical Ashtanga yoga, what we refer to here is an 8-limbed system, which comprises of:

Yamas - Ethical Codes

Niyama - Internal observations

Asana - Seat (today its is referred to as postures)

Pranayama - Breath control

Pratyahara - Sense withdrawal

Dharana - Concentration

Dhyana- Meditation

Samadhi - Bliss

The teachings of Patanjali have created a bridge and an integration between the physical practice of modern Western yoga and the philosophical practises of the East. In this book, we are going to look pacifically at the Yamas and the Niyamas of which each has five.

Ahimsa, Satya, Asteya, Brahmacharya, and Aparigraha are the five Yamas.

Saucha, Santosha, Tapas, Svadiyaha, and Ishvara Pranishana are the five Niyamas,

We are going to learn what they are and how to apply these teachings to our daily lives to take a closer step towards living a life full of lightness.

Day 1

"GRATITUDE UNLOCKS THE
FULLNESS OF LIFE. IT TURNS
WHAT WE HAVE INTO ENOUGH,
AND MORE. IT TURNS DENIAL
INTO ACCEPTANCE, CHAOS TO
ORDER, CONFUSION TO CLARITY.
IT CAN TURN A MEAL INTO A
FEAST, A HOUSE INTO A HOME, A
STRANGER INTO A FRIEND.
"MELODY BEATTIE

Our first lesson is my favourite and a fantastic place to start. The teaching of *Santosha,* which means contentment.

I used to spend all my time looking at my neighbour's garden. I would look at what others have and, in doing so, think about what I don't have. I would look in magazines and on social media and be left with a sense of lack. Lack is not a vibration that I enjoy feeling; lack sends me into a downward spiral of low vibrational thoughts and feelings and, in doing so, limits my ability to receive.

When I was in the darkest, heaviest places of my life, it was the practice of gratitude that helped me stay afloat. I would take myself out of my dark hole and go on a walk and take a note of gratitude for everything I could see: the trees, the park bench, the sky, the sound of the bird, a roof over my head, a meal in my belly, a coat to keep me warm.

While backpacking, my girlfriends and I were in the Philippines and had trekked through the island to a waterfall. We hadn't been prepared and brought no supplies with us—maybe some water but nothing else. When we arrived, not only was nature at its finest, but a local woman struck up a conversation with us. She had not much and plenty of children, and after realising we had no food, she was adamant that she let her feed us with the few biscuits and sandwiches that she had for her own family. This woman was by no means a woman of great wealth, but her sun-kissed face and smile and her generosity left a mark on me. A woman who has nothing but love gave four girls a few biscuits and turned it into a feast.

We can turn what we have into enough and so much more if only we learn the art of contentment and gratitude. Can you practise taking what you have, perhaps the job that you don't like, and being thankful to have a job that pays your bills? Can you take your life and find gratitude for what is in front of you, seeing how much you already have, and let it be enough today?

To practise *Santosha* today, you are going to start by listing 10 things you are grateful for and why.
Then, going forward, every morning you will start by listing 3 things you are grateful for without repeating yourself. Get creative with your gratitude!

Here is an example.

1. Today I am grateful for the bus driver. Without his dedication to his job, I wouldn't make it to work.
2. I am grateful for my boss; their management helps me to work harder and progress.
3. I am grateful for the sound of laughter from my nephew, his giggles remind me to play and have fun in life.

Take a notebook or your notepad on your phone, maybe even a voice note, and start unlocking your gratitude today!

Day 2

"TRUE AHIMSA SHOULD MEAN A COMPLETE FREEDOM FROM ILL-WILL AND ANGER AND HATE AND AN OVERFLOWING LOVE FOR ALL."

Mahatma Gandhi

Ahimsa is a common word thrown around the yogic world, and it means non-violence.

The world is full of physical violence, and Mahatma Gandhi is infamous for his *tapas* (disciple) to protest from a place of love and not from a place of violence. I want to take this teaching of *ahimsa* and move it away from the physical violence aspect and into the subtle violence that we do to ourselves.

At one point in my life, I blacked out all the mirrors in my room. My reflection would cause panic attacks and mental violence as I would verbally attack myself with what I saw in my mirror. I was instilled with the notion that happiness was based on appearance and that in order to be someone, I had to look a certain way. I would terrorise my mind with thoughts of ugliness, I was violent to myself with the words that I told myself, not knowing that words hold power.

In *"The Hidden Messages in Water,"* by Dr. Masaru Emoto, a Japanese scientist proves the power our thoughts have on our wellbeing. By placing rice into three jars of water and repeating words of kindness and love to one, nothing to the second, and words of hate to the third container of rice, the outcome is astonishing. The water of love survives and thrives, the jar of abandonment starts to diminish, and the rice with the words of hate turns black and rots away.

You are no different from the jars of rice and water. The words you tell yourself have the same effect as the words repeated to rice and believe me, you are beautiful, unique and worthy of your own kindness and loving thoughts.

Do you look at the clouds and judge them, or do you just allow them to be a beautiful, unique shape? We create the biggest violence on ourselves with the words we tell ourselves, and today I ask you to stop and start paying attention to the limiting beliefs that you place upon yourself. You deserve to be filled with words of love and encouragement. As you realise you are a child of this earth and as you appreciate the shape of nature, can you learn to appreciate yourself?

I began the task of valuing myself by embracing nonviolence and began with my internal dialogue. Every time I heard my negative self-talk, I would replace it with 3 positives.

Today's task is something I ask all of my students to do, and it can often be difficult at first. If this is true for you, it is ok. Remember,   this is a practice not a perfection!

Today I ask you to write a list of 3 things you value about yourself.

Every day, along with your list of 3 daily gratitudes, you will add one thing you value about yourself.

Here is an example:

1.   I value my ability to listen to others without creating judgement.
2.   I value my ability to organise groups with efficiency and ease for my peers
3.   I value my skills and love as a mother. I may not always get it right, but I always do it with love.

You are good enough, and it is time to value your worth today!

Day 3

. . . .

"YOU WEAR A MASK FOR SO LONG, YOU FORGET WHO YOU WERE BENEATH IT."

Alan Moore, <u>V for Vendetta</u>

Satya comes from the Sanskrit word 'sat' which literally translates as 'true essence' or 'true nature'. *Satya* is knowing our truth beyond the changing, letting go of the 'I," and realising we are something bigger, or seeing "I" as more than just a physical being. *Satya* invites us to become honest with our truth, with who we really are, and realise we are not our thoughts.

As we saw yesterday, our thoughts have the ability to dim our flame. Let's just say I think I am not good at yoga *asana* (postures) because I have tight hamstrings. Just because I think it does not mean it is true, and the teacher, I'm certain, does not see me as bad at yoga *asana* even if I told myself this belief.

In the yoga sutras, Patanjali teaches us that yoga is the stilling of the fluctuations of the mind. The goal of yoga is thus to control the mind and learn to discriminate between what is truth and what is an illusion of our own perception.

While in Morocco, after a Vipassana (a 10-day silent meditation course, the word itself meaning insight), I remember feeling so connected to the vibrations of myself that every time I moved, I could feel the water flowing within me; when I sat down, I was so still, I could feel all the vibrations and the fluctuations of the people around me. I became aware of the constant movement, or *anicca,* the impermanence of life. I began to have insight into my own *anicca* and witnessed that life is a constant ebb and flow; it is never still, and we are just big masses of energies that vibrate with our emotions. I embraced the teaching of *Satya,* and I began to see my pain as a passing moment, for that is the truth. Like the sea that laps up on the shore, it constantly melts back into the belly of the sea. Like the breath that comes into your body, it goes straight back out.

Before I had this awareness, I was addicted to creating a perfect Bryony as a person who was fixed in a shape. But then my eyes were opened, and now I see that Bryony is the name of a living, vibrating light of love and movement.

Today's practice is to see you for who you are, and we are going to do a little bit of meditation.

I want you to find a quiet place and sit comfortably with as straight a spine as possible. When you have made all necessary adjustments to your seat, allow your eyes to close and your palms to rest on your legs. Bring your awareness to your breath and deepen into it. Take a big breath in through your nose, pause and hold your breath for a moment, and then release the breath out of your mouth. Repeat this two more times. Begin to breathe in and out through your nose. Just watch the breath, moving in through the nose and out. What can you sense or feel as the breath passes in and out? Warmth, coolness, sounds? Just continue to watch the passage of breath. Relax into the breath. Relax your legs, pelvis, belly, chest, arms and neck; let your body soften with every breath. Now just allow yourself to be. Let go of your name, let go of your job, let go of your race, and let go of your family. Let all your labels go, and just allow yourself to be. Be the breath. Watch the breath. Feel the breath. Let go of the thoughts as they pass, and come back to just being you. Be you without anyone telling you who or what that is. AND just breathe. Do this meditation for 10–20 minutes and journal your experience.

Day 4

JESUS CHRIST KNEW HE WAS GOD. SO WAKE UP AND FIND OUT EVENTUALLY WHO YOU REALLY ARE. IN OUR CULTURE, OF COURSE, THEY'LL SAY YOU'RE CRAZY AND YOU'RE BLASPHEMOUS, AND THEY'LL EITHER PUT YOU IN JAIL OR IN A NUT HOUSE (WHICH IS PRETTY MUCH THE SAME THING). HOWEVER IF YOU WAKE UP IN INDIA AND TELL YOUR FRIENDS AND RELATIONS, 'MY GOODNESS, I'VE JUST DISCOVERED THAT I'M GOD,' THEY'LL LAUGH AND SAY, 'OH, CONGRATULATIONS, AT LAST YOU FOUND OUT."

Alan Wilson Watts, The Essential Alan Watts

There is a difference between the words purity and cleanliness. But both are definitions of *Saucha*.

The yoga sutras ask us to practise cleanliness on the path to bliss. In theory, it seems simple: wash your hair, wash your body, and don't wear clothes with stains. However, let us throw into the mix the word "purity," which for me has a much more holy and richer context.

I was guilty in my early teens and twenties of living in a horrifically messy, dark room. The clothes lived on the floor, the bed was never made, and space, what space! I had the excuse that it was an organised mess, but all it really was was a reflection of the clutter in my mind. I was depressed, and my external space was a reflection of this.

On the road to my healing, I made a commitment to myself that clothes and other items would be returned to their homes before I went to bed. The bed would be made, and dishes would never be left in the sink. It was not a daunting task at all and never became one. It was a respect that I grew for myself and my things. Through this simple process, my life became brighter. Before I sit down to do work, I clean; when I enter my house, my things are in their place, which gives me space to breathe, room to see, and room to think clearly.

In Bali, especially Ubud, I love that before you step into a shop or some cafes, you remove your shoes. A simple act, but one that makes so much sense: why drag your dirt into someone else's space? The shops often have white tile floors, which are brightly lit and have a breath of cleanliness, a beautiful ritual of respect.

Do we not respect that same level of cleanliness when we recognise that we are but a part of life? Our task for today is to create a new habit of external cleanliness. I ask you to take a moment to reflect on your daily occurrences and notice areas where perhaps I can do better.

Perhaps your car needs an internal or external cleaning, your bathroom is full of half-empty bottles, your workspace, or something else. Choose an area of your life and commit to taking time to create space with *saucha*.

The thought can seem heavy, cleaning has this level of chore or duty behind it; can you change that negative approach to one of respect? It never really takes that long to pick up our things off the floor or put the dishes away; it's more the thought of doing it that requires more energy than the actual doing!

Make a commitment to make a new habit and clean your life, clean your mind, and find some space today.

Day 5

"THE MAIN PROBLEM WITH THIS GREAT OBSESSION FOR SAVING TIME IS VERY SIMPLE: YOU CAN'T SAVE TIME. YOU CAN ONLY SPEND IT. BUT YOU CAN SPEND IT WISELY OR FOOLISHLY."

Benjamin Hoff, The Tao of Pooh

Asteya means non-stealing. I hope by now you know it is wrong to steal, something most of us learned in our toddler years.

I used to steal every day. I didn't steal money or clothes or lipsticks; I stole my happiness. I stole my time, and I stole my own freedom. I would look at other people and steal their moments unbeknownst to them; I would be comparing myself to them. How does my life look compared to the stranger I don't even know? I would compare everything, from the sizes of my thighs to work and my asana practice, it was all about looking outside of me, leading to a tired mind of heaviness and illusions.

As the world of technology advances, social media began to creep in, and more and more our heads and shoulders began to droop as we spent time bouncing through Instagram, Facebook, and any new app that was on the market. I have had many friends, family members, and students, myself included, stress at one point how these social media platforms make them feel small, unworthy, and as if there is no space for them to do what they want to do in this world. I am not here to speak against social media, but I am here to ask you about your relationship with social media. Sometimes we don't even realise that we have a relationship until the question is asked.

My question for you is, How long are you spending scrolling mindlessly on these apps and how do they make you feel? There was a point when I realised that certain people who were coming up on my feed did not make me feel good. An awareness to have at this moment is that this is most certainly not about judging our neighbours, but witnessing what we ourselves feel in these moments. Do I feel a reaction to this? A reaction could be judgment, anger, sadness, or anxiety. If this is happening, then why do you put yourself in that position? This is a form of *asteya*- stealing from your truth and from the other person's prerogative. If you follow people who make you feel small, not good enough, and stop you from following your dreams, then why not for now take them off your feed? Ask yourself, "Does it serve me to feel like this?"

I encourage you to follow people who inspire you, lift you up, and make you smile. Again, I stress that this is not about what other people are doing but simply about honouring your needs at this time.

We can get lost in the scrolls of illusions, as social media is a filtered life. People show you what they want you to see; we must remember this, especially if you feel limited in your own talents while on these platforms.

The time spent scrolling could be used to do the things you put aside, like your secret love of painting, writing, singing, or even just watching the world and its magic in front of your very eyes!

To put *asteya* into practice, I am going to ask you to unfollow anyone who, while scrolling, gives you a reaction and limit your scroll time!

Make the effort today to notice how many times you pick up your phone when you could just be present with yourself. If you really want a challenge, for one day put your phone away, turn it off, and just be!

Day 6

....

"I AM ENOUGH.
I AM COMPLETE."

Karen Druker, **I am loved**

There is a teaching called *Brahmacharya*- its direct translation is *to walk with God*, but it is often translated as celibacy, and the watered-down, westernised version is non-excess. My personal understanding and placement in the modern world is the right use of sexual energy.

You may be thinking, "How does my sexual energy relate to yoga?" It is a very valid question, but through our practice of yoga, cannot we help grow an intimacy with our own being? A sense of value starts to creep up as we start to quiet the stirring thoughts and realise and witness that I am enough.

I remember my first A-HA moment of this in a yoga asana class. I was struggling severely with any sense of confidence, especially in regard to image. I would look in the mirror and pick apart every part of me, only seeing what I thought were flaws. One day, early in my yogic journey, I arrived on my mat and began my practice; there were no mirrors, it was just me, my breath, and my mat, and I cried. There was no external judgment, just sensations and feelings that were not warped by a reflection in a mirror. I felt free and limitless. This is one of many experiences that gave me respect for who I truly am.

As we learn to love ourselves, we start to understand how sacred we are. Your body is sacred. You are sacred, and there is no question on this matter. When we don't know this fact to be true, often self-abuse can slip in, directed towards ourselves and each other. There has been a huge movement in recent times as people spoke out about sexual harassment in every corner of the world, from inside the yoga studio, the workplace, home, and so on. No one has the right to take your sexual energy without your consent, but you also have to protect what you give out.

Your task today is to look in the mirror. Naked. Be bare with yourself and see yourself. Really see yourself and practise moving away from what you don't like and practising seeing a sacred being, and you will start to love and appreciate what you see in yourself.

There is a saying, "Fake it till you make it." If this is really hard for you, keep trying; cry if that is what is needed; scream; or giggle; do it every day until you see yourself for who you are. A unique sacred being of love and repeat.

I am enough; I am complete.

Day 7

. . . .

"LIFE MOVES FORWARD. THE OLD LEAVES WITHER, DIE, AND FALL AWAY, AND THE NEW GROWTH EXTENDS FORWARD INTO THE LIGHT."

Bryant McGil

If by now you haven't heard of the Disney musical *"Frozen"* and from that the infamous song "Let it Go," firstly, I envy you, and second, what's your secret?! These words were heartily sung by every child around the globe.

"Let it go, let it go,
That perfect girl is gone.
Here I stand.
In the light of day
Let the storm rage on.
The cold never bothered me anyway!"

I have strong memories of children in Bali, Australia, the UK and even the Philippines walking around in love with these words. What an innocent reminder of the words we all need to hear. Let it go.

Aparigraha can mean non-grasping, non-coveting or non-attachment, in other words, let go. Right now, take a deep breath in and an even deeper breath out. It feels better, right? So can our entire life when we do just that, when we let go.

The more we cling, the more we grasp, and the more we suffer. Clench your jaw real tight, then your neck and into your shoulders, hold your breath, notice how this feels, and now let that go. Let it all go, allow the body to soften, and feel the breath flowing in and out. Life is like this. When we don't learn to surf the current, we struggle.

While living in Athens, Greece, I struggled a lot with moving vehicles. Athens has its' own method when it comes to driving, and for me as an outsider, all I saw was chaos. It caused me anxiety and fear as I resisted the current that flowed there. This resistance limited my freedom and state of mind. A wise woman once reminded me that I could fight the flow or I could let go into it. I can fight this battle and think my way is right. It may be right, but will it help me? Or do I just have to learn to let go of the way things are?

We cling to people, stories, clothing, ideas, and more. We grasp at what we think should be instead of what is.

Today's work is to think of something in your life that holds you back from your own peace of mind. It can be something big or small. Take a moment to let it come to you.

I then ask you to write out what this situation is.

I.e., I think the rules of the roads in Athens are utter chaos, dangerous, and scary.

Now, write how this limits you, i.e.,

It creates tension in my body and mind and stops me from getting around the city with ease.

Next, I want you to close your eyes and see this situation, really feel it, and sense it in your body. Hold on to this vision and just notice.

Now repeat, "*I let go and of ___(your situation/ idea)_____ as I realise that everything is in perfect order. I trust this process, and I trust I am supported by the universe. I am loved, and I am love.*

Repeat it as many times as you need until you feel it in your body.

As Elsa from Frozen sings and our children instruct us: *"Let the storm rage on; the cold never bothered me anyway."* Let go into the storm and just let it be. When we can accept this, we will be free.

Day 8

"WHETHER OUR ACTION IS WHOLESOME OR UNWHOLESOME DEPENDS ON WHETHER THAT ACTION OR DEED ARISES FROM A DISCIPLINED OR UNDISCIPLINED STATE OF MIND. IT IS FELT THAT A DISCIPLINED MIND LEADS TO HAPPINESS AND AN UNDISCIPLINED MIND LEADS TO SUFFERING, AND IN FACT IT IS SAID THAT BRINGING ABOUT DISCIPLINE WITHIN ONE'S MIND IS THE ESSENCE OF THE BUDDHA'S TEACHING."

Dalai Lama XIV, The Art of Happiness

Discipline often gets a bad rap; it can trigger a negative response when we think of being disciplined by parents or teachers. However, discipline is a skill and a mindset that is required to achieve our goals.

Tapas is a Sanskrit word that is included on the path to freedom. It comes from the root word to burn and is translated as austerity or disciple. Like the cake that needs heat to transform from ingredients to a masterpiece, tapas is the teaching of determined effort in transforming ourselves.

Contrary to yesterday's teaching, which asked us to let go, today's teaching asks us to keep going!

When I was meditating in Bali on my first vipassana, I had to apply this teaching; I had no choice but to find discipline. Discipline to stay, discipline to focus, and discipline to do nothing! My mind would wander to memories of the past, replay events, and even play films behind the darkness of my eyes. The events played out like torture, with nothing to do and nowhere to go but to sit still and find stillness. I am not a still person; I was once described as the most colourful rainbow; I am a highly animated, moving, non-still person; but my lack of stillness in meditation was a reflection of my unease with just being with myself, something I was seeking to amend.

Every morning, I awoke and sat, watching my breath pass in and out through the tip of my nose. With determined effort and letting go into the moment, I achieved my goal. I sat, I found stillness, I learned to let go, and I became nothing. I am not saying I achieved this with perfection, but I did find the stillness and the acceptance I was seeking through determined effort, otherwise known as discipline.

Look at your life and at a goal you have in particular; if you have no goal, then I ask you to make one. Maybe your goal is to go to the gym, take a yoga class, spend time with family, take an art class, or even find time to meditate.

Whatever your goal make a determined effort today on the step toward what you want in life.

I find that when I write things out, I hold myself more accountable, so in your journal, pad, or visible paper, write out:

Today I will _____, i.e., meditate for 10 minutes every morning.

And the steps I will take are _____ set my alarm clock earlier to make time for me!

Sign it, date it, and do it, and keep it visible!

Day 9

"WATCH YOUR THOUGHTS, THEY BECOME YOUR WORDS; WATCH YOUR WORDS, THEY BECOME YOUR ACTIONS; WATCH YOUR ACTIONS, THEY BECOME YOUR HABITS; WATCH YOUR HABITS, THEY BECOME YOUR CHARACTER;

__WATCH YOUR CHARACTER, IT__
__BECOMES YOUR DESTINY.__"

LAO TZU

One of the first steps I took on my path of healing and transformation was when my friend introduced me to the book "The Secret". I brushed it off at first, thinking it was whoo whoo nonsense, but then one day, when I was really struggling, I sought comfort in a book store. As I walked around aimlessly, my eyes caught on a book; it was luminous, as if it had a halo of bright light around it, so I picked it up, and to no surprise, it was The Secret, the very book I had rejected. The universe clearly had other plans for me; I bought it and became open to its teachings. The Secret is an advocate for the law of attraction: what we think, so shall be.

One of my favourite teachings, I often say (but I love them all), is *svadhyaya*, which means self-study. The way in which I ask you to invite this into your life is through witnessing.

In school, we learn about atoms and that we as humans are made up of cells; cells are made up of atoms, and these atoms vibrate. The entire universe is vibrating, everything gives off a vibration. Have you ever walked into a room and felt a heaviness or a lightness?

When you hear the term "vibing," you are literally vibrating at a frequency. We vibrate constantly. When this is understood, we understand the law of attraction. What I think I am attracting, what I give off, so I am. If I am vibrating at what I call low vibrational thoughts, i.e., "I am not good enough," then this is radiating out; if I am thinking high vibrational thoughts, i.e., "I am enough and more," then this is in my aura.

New research says we have over 6,000 thoughts a day. Just take that number in; it is a lot, and *Svadhyaya* asks us to witness these thoughts.

As you go about your day, I want you to watch your thoughts and notice your reactions. What vibe are you giving off?

Study what presses your buttons and what makes you smile.

Every time you have a negative reaction, i.e., you bump your head on the open cupboard door, how do you react? Can you practice a new way to react, like laughter?

Note down everything you notice: the event, your reaction, and your new reaction.

If you want to be happy, it starts with you. Be the vibration that you want to attract, and it starts with creating new habits and new reactions.

Day 10

....

"YOU HAVE TWO HOMES
EARTH AND YOUR BODY
TAKE CARE OF THEM "

Somewhere along the way, we humans have forgotten that we are part of this planet. As we distinguished ourselves as the smartest species, we began to separate ourselves from our roots and origin, Mother Earth.

She is the very structure of the ground upon which you lie, sit, or stand right now and has supported you since the moment you were conceived. But this is a love that I fear has become one-sided; the child takes but has forgotten to give back.

Today we reflect back on *Ahimsa,* the teaching of non-violence, and apply it to the home that allows us to be here living this journey, Earth.

I can't recall a moment in particular when my love for and need to protect Mother Earth began, but I do recall always loving animals, and when I was a child, my parents even built a huge kitchen cabinet-sized open hutch for my guinea pigs and rabbits in their living room. In my early twenties, I began to educate myself on the production of animal products and the effects that played out on the environment due to the industry.

I remember the first time the impact of seeing the polluted waters made me feel. In the beautiful jungle of Bali, I swam through a web of dirty nappies, bottles, and human trash. I felt the hurt on my friend's face as he witnessed the destruction of his Greek roots as we took a trip to the sea, which washed in everything from dead dolls, hangers, bottles, and toys. I walk down a beach and pick up cigarette butts one after the other. Earth is beautiful, but we have each paid a price for her destruction, and we can hold no one accountable but ourselves.

Today I ask you to make a commitment to Mother Earth, who is calling out for your love. It is not a laughing matter anymore or a joke to make fun of those who care and protest. The very future of life depends on your attention. If you are unaware of the consequences of the actions of humans, then I invite you to educate yourself. I wish for our children to swim in clean waters, eat clean food, and have a clean future.

I invite you today to make one change. Perhaps you purchase a wooden toothbrush or finally buy a reusable drinking cup. Maybe you make a commitment to only buy loose vegetables and reduce your meat intake. Perhaps you educate yourself on your carbon footprint and make an effort to cycle where you once took the bus. One change will make a difference. On hearing I didn't eat meat while backpacking, a man once said to me, "Your actions won't change the world." Well, I beg to differ, I know that my actions and my voice have impacted more than I could imagine, and so can yours.

What change can you make today to save the home that you have and to protect the future of the children?

Write it down, make a change, and commit to your own growth.

Day 11

"I WILL NOT LET ANYONE WALK THROUGH MY MIND WITH THEIR DIRTY FEET."

Mahatma Gandhi

Hopefully, by now you have started your practice of external cleanliness. Making a determined effort to create a clean space around you as a new habit. As we look once more at the teaching of *Saucha*, or "cleanliness" or "purity," I now invite us to take it from external work to internal work and work at the purification of the mind.

We know that eating junk food is bad for us. We know that if we eat a burger and chips and ice cream and a milkshake and top it off with caramel popcorn, we will feel icky, sluggish, and heavy. We also know that if we repeatedly eat these foods, we will become ill. You can watch "Supersize Me" for reference if you don't believe me! If we know that junk food is bad for us and that in order to get healthy, we need to clean up our diet, then we must also wake up and see that our junk thoughts will also make us sick.

Why do we feed ourselves junk thoughts?

I was in Indonesia, staying in a luxurious villa surrounded by stunningly kind and beautiful people, and from anyone else's perspective, it would have been an envious experience. However, I went into my suite and saw that I had filled myself with junk food thoughts. I saw my reflection and talked myself down and rotten until I was in a state of hysteria. I can't tell you how powerful your thoughts are over your happiness. A dear friend found me and she held me, and although she could not understand why I was being so hurtful to myself, she asked me why I talk to myself like I am some sort of monster.

After years of never believing in myself, I had literally talked myself into depression and sickness.

I started using affirmations when I was 21 years old. I had already noticed how my mind was filled with junk and that it was detrimental to my happiness. I began the tedious job of purifying my mind. I created a mental diet.

I invite you today to take your mind on a cleanse, to get junk thoughts out and replace them with powerful super thoughts!

As we see how lovely it is to walk into a clean room, our minds are the same. A clean mind is a wonderful place to dwell.

Today, by putting *ahimsa* (non-violence), *svadihyaya* (self-study) and *saucha* into practise I want you to really witness every time you have a junk food thought.

Notice when you wake up with an ache and you say "Ugh, my old body", when you see something someone else has and you judge, whatever it is, then notice, stop, and say something nice to yourself. Instead of saying, "Ugh, my old tired body", stop, breathe and say something kind. "I love you body; thank you for carrying me through all of my life experiences."

Cleanse your mind, and the world will literally change in front of you. Are you ready?

Day 12

"WHO ARE YOU TO JUDGE THE LIFE I LIVE?
I KNOW I'M NOT PERFECT
-AND I DON'T LIVE TO BE-
BUT BEFORE YOU START
POINTING FINGERS...
MAKE SURE YOU HANDS ARE
CLEAN!"

Bob Marley

When traveling through Southeast Asia, I promise you that wherever you go, there is always a reggae bar with Bob Marley music being played for all to hear, and they can normally guarantee a good time. Bob Marley shared the song and its lyrics

"One Love, One Heart
Let's get together and feel all right"

We are all part of this Earth, we came from this Earth, and we will go back to it when our time here is over. We are all creatures of creation and come from the same source. I invite you to see this as love.

The very first practice I asked you to start with was gratitude, and by now your list should be growing and growing with all the beautiful things around you. The teaching of *santosha,* or contentment, which can mean a place of balance in the mind, is much like the experience of my first great love, which felt like complete balance.

When we live our lives in a state of *santosha,* we can start to see love everywhere.

Bob Marley invited us to be in love with all; it is not luck that his songs still play out today across the world; it is because he sang the truth. What stops us from seeing and being in a state of oneness? What stops us from seeing each other as entities of love?

As humans, we are quick to judge others, but judging is an act of not knowing. We judge what we do not understand. People hurt us, but most of the time their actions are an outward manifestation of hurt within their own lives.

Today I want you to play a game. With everyone you encounter, I want you to see them as love beings. Remember when you were a kid and you could imagine anything as possible? Then why is it not possible to see all beings as beings of love.

When the barrister makes you coffee, see them as a being of this earth, a being of love. In a crowded room, envision everyone as a being who is a child of this earth, a child who needs to be nurtured and loved. If you are irritated by someone or judging someone, stop and see them as a child of love.

Be creative; maybe you just see a hug monster hugging them and filling them with love. Maybe you just shower them in love, or maybe you can see what being of love looks like.

Give it a go. See all beings as one great big love being, one love, one heart.

Day 13

··

"IN AN ERA WHERE WOMEN UNDRESS THEIR OUTFITS & GIVE THEIR BODIES SO CARELESSLY, BECOME THE RARE WILD WOMAN THAT UNDRESSES HER MIND AND SOUL & KNOWS THE WORTH OF WHAT SHE HAS TO OFFER."

Nikki Rowe

I was so afraid of not being liked that I would give myself panic attacks. I would create all these different scenarios in my head about what people thought or would think about me; I literally suffocated myself to the point of not breathing while living in the shadow of others.

Satya, as we looked at it, means true essence, knowing the self beyond the changing self. Exploring this teaching further, let us also see it as living and stepping into the boldest, raddest, unapologetic love beings of who we are.

I often hear people (including myself) express the fear of saying or doing the things they really want to say or do. Why? Why do we block our own authenticity? Is it because we are scared to be seen, heard, or judged? People will always judge. You can allow that fact to rule your life, or you can do you any way and live an adventurous life of experiences!

In Berne Brown's worldwide successful Ted Talk, she researched the power of vulnerability, and from her research, she discovered the happiest people were those who were vulnerable, those who took risks, and those who were authentic to their needs and wants. If research is telling you that doing what you really want and being open will actually make you happier, then why are you still worried about the thoughts of others? Those who can not keep up with your brilliance will fade away, and those who see you for who you are will flock to you like kids to a candy store.

The term for a yoga practise is *sadhana;* it means the spiritual path of knowing one's self, and this is the path of yoga. As we still our minds, draw our minds towards ourselves, and know who we are and what we want in life, we are better able to go out and get those things.

To be authentic in your life, what does that even look like for you? What does this mean for you? Maybe wearing a style of clothing you identify with is something you've been scared to wear due to a fear of being seen and judged. Maybe it's learning to say no to the extra workload and standing up for your mental health. *Satya* invites you to be you, exactly as you are today.

Your task today is to be authentic to yourself and make choices for you, not for your ego, for your family, or for likes on social media. Act with love, compassion, and kindness in your heart towards those around you and twice as much toward yourself.

When you live a life of authenticity, your shoulders will be free of the burden of shadows. You were born for brilliance, but you can't do it in the shadow of others.

Day 14

"*TO LIVE IS THE RAREST THING IN THE WORLD. MOST PEOPLE EXIST, THAT IS ALL.*"

Oscar Wilde

As we come to our final lesson, I hope that you have enjoyed the process of taking the teachings of the yamas and niyamas of the yoga sutras and applying them as principles in your life. I am certain that you found some tasks a breeze, some challenging, and some you skipped completely.

The last teaching is Ishvara Pranidhana. Ishvara means Lord, and pranidhana means surrender—surrender to the Lord. If we replace the word Lord with love, Ishvara Pranidhana then means surrender to love.

A few days ago, I asked you to see love in all beings; now, I ask you to see love in all experiences. You are a child of this world, and all children deserve love, happiness, and abundance. Children also need schooling and education to learn, grow, and develop.

Your experiences, good and bad, are educational lessons in your own self-growth. If I had not experienced all the pain and suffering that I did, then I could not have evolved, grown, or even felt the compassion and understanding of others that I do today.

So I ask you to learn to trust and surrender to all of your experiences, especially your challenges. Trust that you are loved, and trust that you are being divinely led on a path to greatness.

On your dark days, surrender to the love of your friends and family. They love you, and they want to help you. On your most adventurous days, surrender to the love of the moment, try not to think it has to be any different and recognise that it is perfect as it is.

When we start to apply all of these teachings daily, our mindsets will literally shift. Remember when we talked about vibrations? You will vibrate at a new frequency, and you will find more balance and happiness in your life. Surrender to the days when the clouds roll back in because they will. We repeat our challenges until we really have overcome them, so try not to feel disheartened when your old habits creep back in. When the junk thoughts take over and the gratitude light seems dim, surrender to love once more and begin again.

Find love within yourself. When you see how much of a gift you are on this earth, you will radiate like the sun, but no one can show you; you must surrender to yourself.

Today's task is to remember this truth. You are loved, and that love is there for you. Love is around you, and love helps you grow. As you see love in others and in creation, you will see that you are part of it all and that you deserve your own love.

About the Author

Bryony's spiritual journey began when she packed her bags and took to traveling the world in her early 20s, knowing there had to be more to life than working like she had been socially conditioned to do. She began to let herself learn from nature, different religions and cultures, strangers, and her spiritual teachers. It was at this time, when she had been suffering from illness and depression, that she took back her power and healed herself through the teachings of yoga and more profoundly, meditation.

Bryony has over 1500 hours of yoga teacher training certifications, and she deeply believes that yoga can enhance and radically transform the lives of all those who choose to walk this path.

Connect with Bryony at yogabstudio.com or @yogabstudio

A little note

Never give up on what you dream of. I have always wanted to write a book, and here it is. I am not even sure who will find this little book of wisdom, but for those of you who have, thank you for taking the time to read my words.

Thank you to everyone who has ever supported me, from my very first ballet teacher, Linda, who believed in me, to the students who come to my classes and continue to listen to what I have to share.

I am blessed because of you, and I thank you from the bottom of my heart.

All my love,

B x